NOT ALL HANDS FEED YOU

A Poetic Memoir

M. E. ROBINSON

EDITOR: Stacey Robinson (Kya Publishing)
PAGE / EBOOK DESIGNER: Osamudiamenabdu Suleiman (Nigeria)
COVER DESIGNER: Chamika Dinesha
PAGE ART: Rhiza Jennina Dizon (Philippines)
CONTRIBUTIONS: ElevatedWaves Publishing Corp.

PUBLISHER: M. E. Robinson Publishing (Cleveland, Ohio)

ISBN (Paperback): 979-8-9922447-0-0
ISBN (Ebook): 979-8-9922447-1-7

Library of Congress Control Number: 2024926858
Printed in the United States of America

For the little girls who looked to the wrong hands for sustenance,
and the full women they became once they knew better.

CONTENTS

INTRODUCTION

I was born in 1997, to a strung-out mother and a father who never knew I was his child. I used to think of the day I was born as the unluckiest day there was, because of everything that followed.

Born with drugs in my system and not a fit parent in sight, I was taken in by my family on my mother's side. While in their care, I was verbally, mentally, and physically abused for the first sixteen years of my life, and intermittently in the years to follow. In addition to that, I went to Juvie twice before the age of thirteen and spent most of my youth trying to get Child Protective Services (CPS) to believe me when I told them about the abuse I endured.

The only things that brought me happiness during those times were visits to my great-grandmother Tiny's house (before she passed), school, books, writing, and daydreaming about the life I would have once I escaped. At sixteen, I was blessed to finally encounter a CPS caseworker that saw my living situation for what it was, and I was granted my request to go to foster care.

At this time, I thought I had finally escaped and was on my way to greater things—boy, was I wrong! I went into my new living situation unhealed and rebellious. Before long, I ended up pregnant by a boy who used my experiences against me, and I was kicked out of my first foster home. At that point I thought, "This is it! Everyone was right about me and the foster care system."

Again, I was wrong!

Once I had a (regretful) abortion, I was given a second chance at having a family. The only problem was, I was even more unhealed and rebellious. Despite this, I was well taken care of and loved until the day I left that household.

After I was emancipated from foster care, I spent the first year of my adulthood struggling, angry, and depressed. Without genuine support or proper help, I often asked myself, "What is the point of being here?"

By the age of nineteen, I decided I wanted better for myself, so I began to focus on healing and transforming myself. Slowly, —and I do mean slowly—, I began to work on my boundaries, temperament, perspective, and my relationship with God, as well as my spiritual connection. I did all of this while keeping faith and doing my best to ignore obstacles or individuals that said I could never do it.

It was not an easy path—forgiving the transgressions of others, as well as my own—however, I did it and I continue to progress to this day. There was a time I couldn't imagine openly sharing my experiences, or realizing that I am past them. Yet here I sit, putting my pain to paper and feeling free as I do so.

I cannot say I did it alone, because I most certainly did not. I found kindness and love in strangers, caseworkers, teachers, mentors, therapists, friends, foster parents, a few family members, and most importantly God and my ancestors. Even before I found those things within myself. I am grateful to note that while I have encountered many a hand that did not feed me, I have also encountered even more that did, will, and do. All the same, each hand I encountered has made me the woman I am today, and is deserving of acknowledgment.

I found that the best way for me to give that acknowledgement was to write this collection of poems. Additionally, I would be remiss if I did not mention that I both believe God to be the highest power, and practice Spirituality. It is my belief that using my intuitive gifts and connecting with my ancestral line is not separate from my belief in God, but a part of it. I wanted to explain this, in case you as the reader found yourself curious.

Finally, I want to say *thank you* to whomever is reading this, for allowing me the opportunity to share my story with you. I pray that your mind, body, and soul are not only fed, but full! And if not? I pray that you at least possess the faith that one day they will be.

HAND ME DOWNS

On the day the world heard my first cry
My ancestors wept
Not for joy
But, for me
For they knew
That it was I
Who was next in line
To be handed the things—
They too were handed
The very things that had survived
Decades
Generations
Them
My ancestors wept
As they bore witness
To all the—
Pain
Jealousy
Malice
Confusion
And most of all—

The rage

Being passed
Hand to hand
Soul to soul
Them to me
Not a break to be taken
Nor a second to waste

Yes
On the day the world heard my first cry
My ancestors wept
Not for joy
But, for me

ROCK WAS A DRUG, NOT A VERB

If only I had been small
Small enough to be held easily

If only I had been fragile
Fragile enough to be protected fiercely

If only I had been important
Important enough to be thought of

If only I had been expensive
Expensive enough to be worked for

If only I had been addictive
Addictive enough to keep you bound

If only

If only I had been those things
Maybe then you would have—
Soothed
Cradled
Rocked
Maybe, even

Mothered
Me

FUMBLED BY THE HANDS OF THE SYSTEM

Treated like cargo
None too precious

Just something to pick up
And drop off

Handled so carelessly
So improperly

Far too burdensome
Far too inconvenient

For the system
The very system that failed

Failed to treat me like a human
Like a baby

No

In the system's hands
I was treated like cargo

None too precious

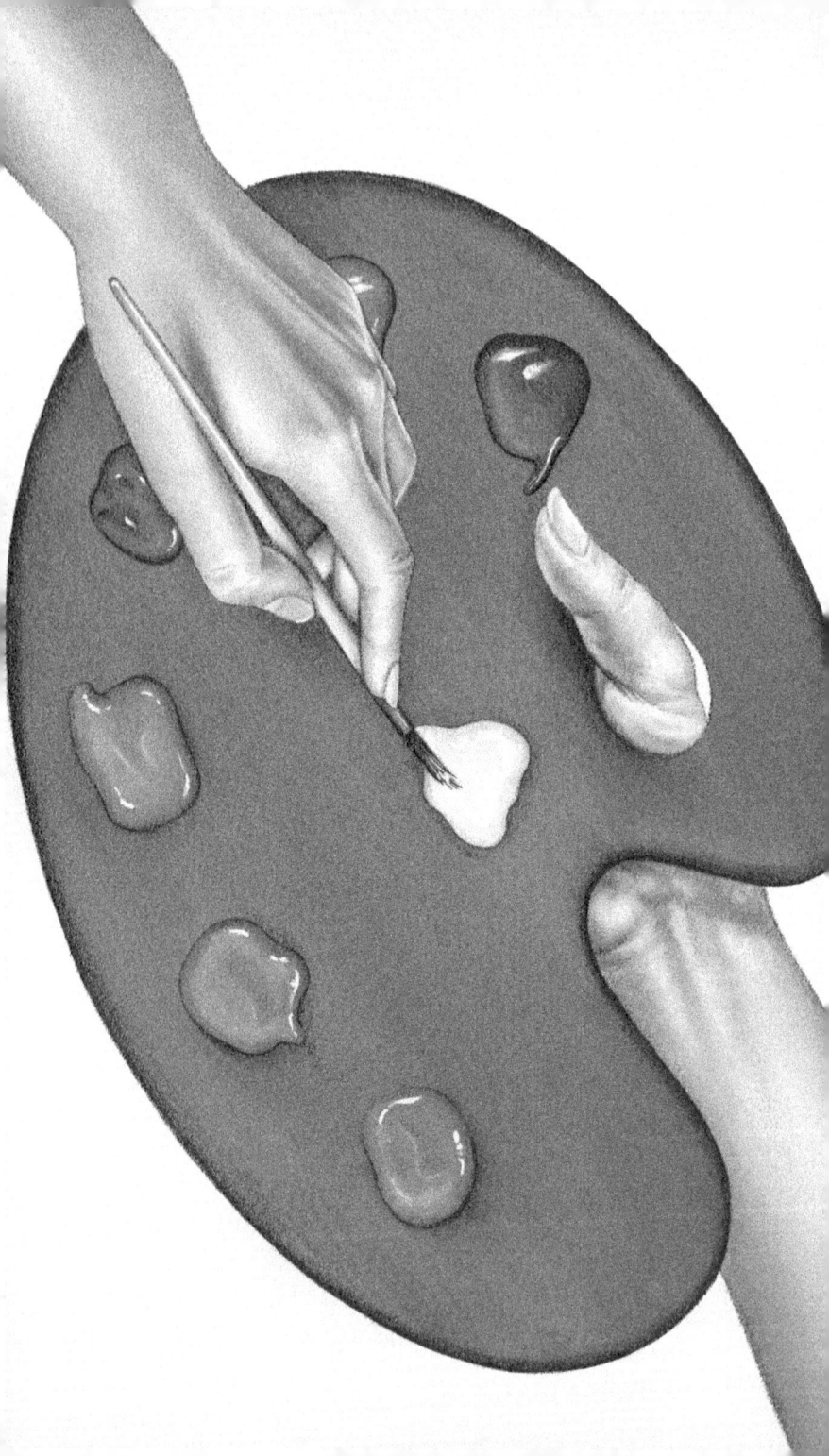

A MUSE AT YOUR FINGERTIPS

Nails
Beautiful
Sharp

Carving red into yellow skin

Fingers
Nimble
Strong

Pinching memories across pouted lips

Palms
Artful
Heavy

Slapping violet and black across delicate features

Hands
Carving
Pinching
Slapping

A canvas
A masterpiece

A child

TINY('S) TOUCH

My soul knew a touch
Unlike any other

A touch as silent as the butterflies
were when landing on your prized magnolias

A touch as sweet as the sugar I was begrudgingly
allowed to dump in my morning Cheerios

A touch as comforting as the smell of that special grease
you taught me to use moderately on your scalp

A touch as solid as the wardrobe
that held your collection of housecoats

A touch as bold as me eating the last banana
that you specifically said not to

A touch as soothing as your voice
reading *Cat in the Hat* for the millionth time

A touch as soft as your beautiful snores lulling me
to my own

A touch as lovely as the bows you'd
put on my ponytails for First Sundays

A touch as welcome as the
"*I'm sick of you; you're going to your great grandma's house*" days.

A touch as fierce as the protection you reserved
for the little girl no one did right by.

Yes
My soul knew a touch.
Unlike any other.

Taken entirely too soon.

A touch that was everything
And anything

But tiny.

THE CLOCK'S HANDS TOLD THE LIE

The clock hands struck
Twelve

An even number
Even as the four pairs of eyes bearing witness
To the misunderstanding
Misinterpretation, even

The clock hands struck
Twelve

An abundant number
Abundant as the eighteen cases on the docket
To be tried
Judged, even

The clock hands struck
Twelve

A divisible number
Divisible by three to be exact
Three being the number of minutes it took
To walk down that hallway of shame
Chagrin, even

The clock hands struck
Twelve

A terrible number
Though
Not nearly as terrible as ninety-six
Ninety-six being the number of days
Days it took be processed.

Labeled.
Treated.
As a problem
As a delinquent, even.

But not once
As a Victim.

DOING THE HAMBONE ON ME

You're going to be just like your mother
Look at how fat you are
I locked her in her room because she's on punishment

SLAP

I hate you
This is why I don't buy you anything
Get out of my sight

SLAP

You should be on medication
I'm not coming to your graduation
My grandmother begged me to take you in

SLAP

All you do is lie
You'll never amount to anything good
Stop crying before I give you something to cry about

SLAP

If you try to eat at school, I'll know
Look at what you've done
Magic City has a pole waiting just for you

SLAP

Her SSI check is coming next week;
I'll get your Jordan's then
You're a crack baby
Nobody cares about your birthday

SLAP

You don't know what abuse is
That caseworker won't believe a word you say
I bought her a winter coat; I don't know why she's
wearing a hoodie to school

SLAP

You put those bruises on yourself
Wipe that smirk off your face
Girls get raped or worse in foster care you know

Slap
Slap
SLAP

My Body
My Mind
My Soul
Willing victims to their rhythmic percussion

My Existence
My Livelihood
My Childhood
Forced to dance to the beat of their cruelty,
without interruption

MY LOVER HELD ME

My lover had a way
A way of sweeping all the girls off their feet
Quickly.

How could they have known?
Known that the fall into his love could be breathtaking
Painful.

My lover had a way
A way of whispering in all the girls' ears
Why didn't they hear?

Truly hear.
The syllables that were cloyingly sweet
Only to be savored as nothing.

I did

I heard
I swallowed
I vomited
That nothing.

Because my lover had a way
A way of holding every girl just right
Except me.

It was me
That my lover held, in the only way he could

Down.

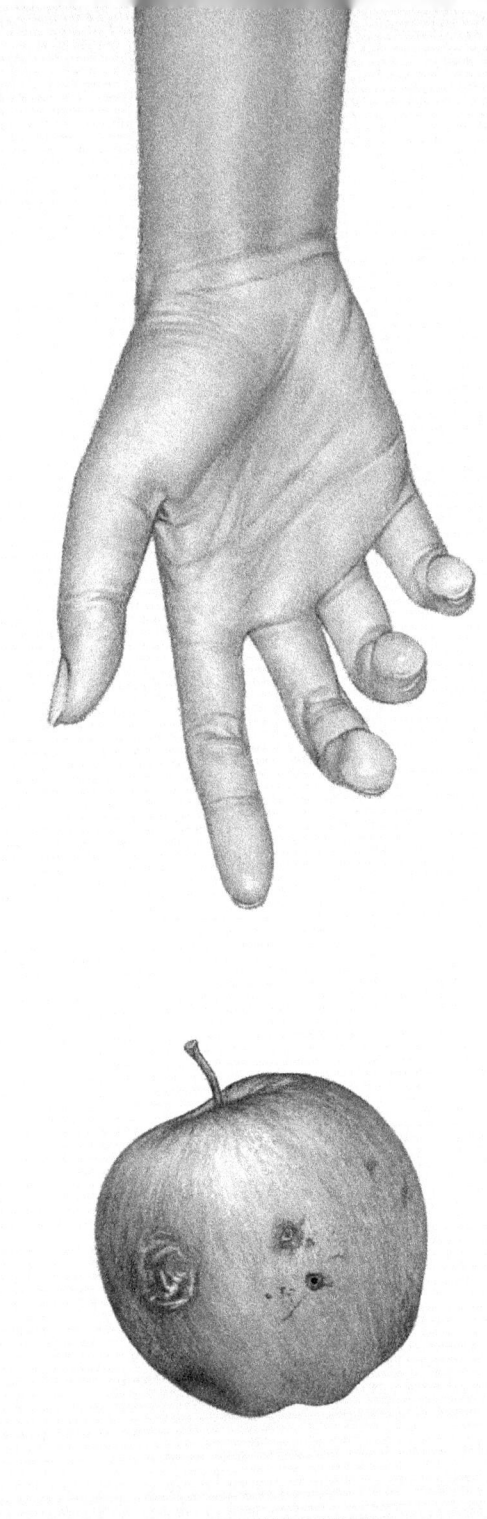

PLUCKED BUT NOT YET PICKED

Spotted

A lone apple

On an otherwise bare—

Forgotten tree

Ripe

Ready

Waiting

For Anyone

And there you were

Ravenous

Though, only briefly

For when you plucked it, distaste set in

This apple wasn't to your liking

Far too bruised

Far too small

Growing even smaller as it fell from your fingers

Far from its tree

And even farther from you

A STRANGER SCRUBBED IN

Five minutes.
Five minutes was all it took
Took for a stranger's hands to be clean enough
To touch my body
My impurity
My shame

Five minutes.
Five minutes was all it took
Took for a stranger's hands to be sneaky enough
To snatch away my youth
My naivety
My optimism

Five minutes.
Five minutes was all it took
Took for a stranger's hands to be demanding enough
To grab my ankles
My uncertainty
My "*No.*"

Five minutes.
Five minutes was all it took
Took for a stranger to know enough
Know enough to judge
To finalize
To kill.

Five minutes.
Five minutes was all it took
For a stranger to scrub

For me, it'll be an eternity.

PLACED ON MY FIRST PEDESTAL

We were standing
You waiting
Me stalling
The floor littered with the broken eggshells
I'd been walking on
Their white stained by dried tears
Tears we both knew to be mine

Go on
You said

Step up
I heard

Yet I didn't understand
Understand how I could step away
From what was comfortable
Familiar
Deserved

So, I remained
Still
Stubborn

With a demeanor full of understanding
You placed your determination
in the small of my defeat

Moving me forward
You encircled my burdens with your grace and lifted
My fear protesting and kicking

Nonetheless
You positioned my flaws on a surface
shined with acceptance
All the while using your strength to stabilize
my trembling disbelief

You did it
You said

We both knew I hadn't
Neither of us said so

Once again, we stood
You, amongst my mess
Me, towering above it

You deserve to be there
You said

As you nudged my self-esteem up from its usual bow
For this act, you used what I'd find to be the greatest
kindness

Your love

TORN TO PIECES

Your approval
Once strong, evident
Turned flimsy, understated
Became
Susceptible to damage

The kind of Damage—
Entitlement
Opposition
And even
Misplaced blame

Can cause

You see
I didn't yet know
How to appreciate
How to submit
How to relax

Yet I knew
How to question
How to revolt
How to destroy

Your approval
Flimsy, understated
Was like paper in careless hands
Easily torn, easily scattered.

CHOKING OUT DREAMS

Their backhanded compliments
Poised
Swift
Heinous
Wrapped around my skinny confidence

Their untoward opinions
Skilled
Brutal
Overbearing
Pressing down on my bare vulnerability

Their empty promises
Practiced
Unforgiving
Violent
Choking the life out my fragile aspirations

Their intent
Was to —
Restrict
Harm
Murder

Efficiently
Effectively
Effortlessly

Every single dream
I had breathed life into

A PUSH FROM GOD

My child
My beautiful child

I created you
To be the *Love*
For those who lacked it within

I chose you
To be the *Patience*
For those who had frayed their own

My child
My beautiful child

I enabled you
To be the *Change*
For those stalled with stubbornness

I revealed you
To be the *Proof*
For those without belief

My child

I pushed you
To be *Beautiful*
In spite of those who treated you so ugly

GOT A GRIP

Such a pretty little thing
My anger
Lovely as it taunts my attempts at control
Dainty as it steps around my resistance
Beguiling as it steals my peace

Such a pretty little thing
My anger
So pretty
So little
It pains me
Pains me to call it forward
Under the guise of a gentle touch
Only to grip it
Entrap it
Shatter it.

Such a pretty little thing
My anger
Was.

KNEADING FORGIVENESS

I had a taste
For something I'd never had
Never wanted
A taste
For something there was no recipe for
No directions for
Something soft and satiating
Warm and different

Forgiveness

And so
I
Weighed out the pros
Measured out the cons
Poured a cup of compassion
Reserved a dash of tranquility
Used relief to activate
Incorporated each feeling slowly
Dusted the surface of my mind with acceptance

And with patience I began to
Fold
Press
And roll

Forgiveness

Kneading with intention
And anticipation
Kneading until my heart felt full
And free

Satisfied, I
Placed and covered with care
And waited

As forgiveness

Rested
And rose

THUMBING THROUGH LIFE

With restless fingers
I thumbed through
Yet another chapter of life
Wearied
Distracted
Impatient
For it was the ending that I craved
The ending that reads of the climax
I'd reached
Of the fairytale
I'd chased
Of the happiness
I'd found
With restless fingers
I thumbed through
Yet another chapter of life
Unimpressed
Entitled
Foolish
For it was regard that I lacked
For the greatest part of my life's story
The plot.

PAST GRASPING AT STRAWS

I had reached the end
Of my surplus of straws
Panicked and angry
I sulked
Wondering
What do I do now?

And there it was
A glass
Half full
Taunting me
No, coaxing
Coaxing me to have faith
Trust
Motivation

To drink
Drink in its offer
Opportunity
Chance

My mouth
Unbelieving
Set
Dry

Dry with unanswered pleas
Unrewarded attempts
Unquenched thirsts
And yet I see it

A glass
Half full
Asking
No, begging
Me
Of all people, me
To drink
In its optimism
Hope
Salvation

And so, with weak
No, tired
With tired fingers I grasp
Not at
Not for
No
I simply, grasp
The glass
And drink my fill

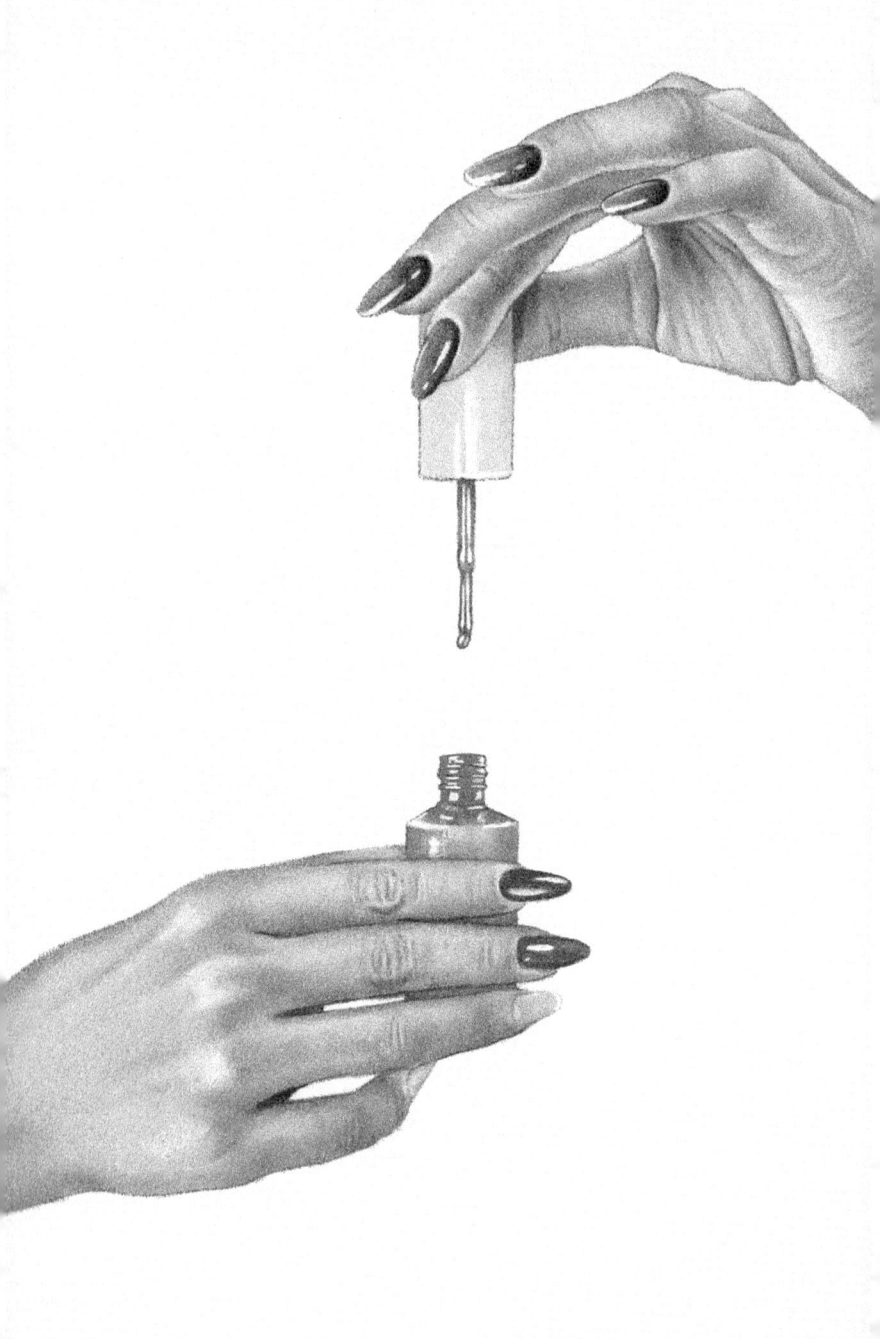

IN NEED OF A MANICURE

My life
Calloused from pressure
Dried from endurance
Roughened from neglect
Unsightly
Withered
This has to change
Life is meant to be beautiful
Smooth
Relaxed
It's time to pamper myself —
The thoughts in my head
As I
Soak my life in desire
Push my life back from defeat
Trim my life of regret
Shape my life to be well rounded
Buff my life with tenderness
Exfoliate my life, utilizing will
Moisturize my life with goals
And finally
I
Polish my life
With the color of celebration

CUTTING THE CAKE FOR OTHERS' SAKE

They said
The cake wasn't mine
For the taking
They said
I couldn't have
As well as eat
The cake
So long I've spent
Cutting morsels
Small
Acceptable
Lowering my appetite
My expectations
Not one complaint on my tongue
As I got the lesser
The portion
Of what I deserved
What I labored for
Salivated for
But, why should I?
Settle?
Settle for a piece
Of what I am due
It is time

Time, I stopped giving
And started taking
Having
Eating
Something
Everything
The Cake.

APPLAUDABLE EFFORTS

I clap
For the women that have tuned their ears
to hear the cries of their inner child
For the women that wear their battle scars
with the confidence of a runway model
For the women that calm storms
instead of weather them

I clap
For the women that both pray
and work for better days
For the women that romanticize
the little things in life
For the women that used their last
to put themselves first

I clap
For the women that dare to dream
with their eyes wide open
For the women that don't hesitate to pour into others
because they are just brimming with abundance
For the women that have walked through fire
and managed to barely break a sweat

I clap
For the women that chose healing over hurting
For the women that chose triumph over failure
For the women that chose life over death

In short
I clap
For the women that are just like me

MY WHOLE WORLD IN HIS HANDS

He's got my whole world in His hands

And in His hands
My world is thriving
The sun never ceases to rise
The harvests are abundant
The grass is the lushest green

And I
Am happy
Yes

He's got my whole world in His hands

And in His hands
My world is safe
The air smells of purpose
The birds chirp with glee
The rain is seldom

And I
Am free
Yes

He's got my whole world in His hands

And I
Am allowed to just be
Yes.

MY HANDS

My hands
Patient as the last apple waiting
to be picked from its tree
Golden as a spoonful of honey melting across
a freshly baked biscuit
Soft as chocolate spreading
on a warm tongue

My hands
Agile as butter seeping
into a pot of simmering grits
Textured as an avocado
lazing through the summer
Strong as the aroma of garlic
sautéing in olive oil

My hands
Pretty as the batter of cornbread
folding into a greased pan
Grateful as a pot of dry mashed potatoes
being revived by heavy cream
Big as the prized pumpkins
at the local county fair

My hands
Selfless as an offer to wash the dishes
after you've finished cooking
Experienced as your grandmother's
well-seasoned cast iron skillet
Comforting as you coming home
to a Crock-Pot meal,
on a cold winter's day

My hands
Provide
Satisfy
Feed.

ACKNOWLEDGEMENTS

With a profound sense of gratitude and respect, I would first like to thank God and my ancestors for not only bestowing upon me a blessed existence, but also the gift of creativity.

Additionally, I would like to thank my tribe: Ja'Von, Simone, Erica, Crystal, Andrae, and Leonard. You all have a permanent place in my heart, for forever and a day.

Lastly, I would like to thank every single individual — known, familiar, or stranger to me — that added to my existence and experience of life.

I am eternally grateful.

ABOUT THE AUTHOR

A passionate writer with a love for poetry, M.E. Robinson is a debut novelist. Drawing inspiration from her traumatic past and upbringing, she transforms her pain into poetry, vulnerably highlighting her transition from a hurt child to a healed adult.

She wrote this collection of poetry with the intent to inspire those who are on their own healing journey, hoping to shed light on the beauty that can come of it. When not writing, she dedicates her time to college - as a culinary student, connecting with fellow veterans, performing at open mic nights, reading, volunteering, and sending *"I'm cooking, are you coming to get a plate?"* texts to her closest friends and family… and they always say "YES!"